Topsy + Tim ™

Green
ACTIVITY BOOK

Jean and Gareth Adamson

Blackie Children's Books

BLACKIE

Published by the Penguin Group
Penguin Books Ltd, 27 Wrights Lane, London W8 5TZ, England
Penguin Books USA Inc., 375 Hudson Street, New York, New York 10014, USA
Penguin Books Australia Ltd, Ringwood, Victoria, Australia
Penguin Books Canada Ltd, 10 Alcorn Avenue, Toronto, Ontario, Canada M4V 3B2
Penguin Books (NZ) Ltd, 182–190 Wairau Road, Auckland 10, New Zealand

Penguin Books Ltd, Registered Offices: Harmondsworth, Middlesex, England

Published by Blackie 1995
1 3 5 7 9 10 8 6 4 2

Copyright © Jean & Gareth Adamson and Penguin Books Limited, 1995
Information text by Carol Watson
Information illustrations by Mike Foster, Maltings Partnership

The moral right of the authors and illustrators has been asserted

Design by Between the Lines, London
Filmset in Century Schoolbook Infant
Made and printed in Great Britain by William Clowes Limited, Beccles and London

A CIP catalogue record for this book is available from the British Library

ISBN 0-216-94095 8 Hbk
ISBN 0-216-94096 6 Pbk

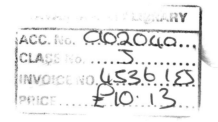

When Topsy and Tim came home from school one Friday afternoon they looked a bit glum.

"What's the matter with you two?" asked Dad.

"Miss Terry says everyone is messing up the world with rubbish and fumes and stuff," said Tim.

"And there are so many people that there is no room left for wild animals and forests," said Topsy.

Threats to our world:

When we cut down forests of trees, we destroy the homes of many animals, birds and plants.

Poisonous smoke from factories pollutes the air and rivers. It makes them dirty.

Oil spilt from ships poisons the oceans and kills sea birds and fish.

Spraying our crops with pesticides kills insects that animals and birds eat.

People drop litter and dump rubbish. This makes our towns dirty, and harms the countryside.

"Miss Terry says we have all got to do something about it,"
said Tim.
"Miss Terry is quite right," said Mummy. "And we could
start doing something this weekend if you like."
Topsy and Tim cheered up and enjoyed their tea.

Next morning, after breakfast, Mummy said, "Today we are going to help our poor old world. We will do the shopping and choose all the things that do it the least harm."
"We will take our old glass jars and bottles to the bottle-bank to be recycled," said Dad, "and our old newspapers, too."

Did you know?

Some aerosol sprays and packaging contain chemicals called CFCs. These destroy the ozone layer which protects us from the sun's harmful rays.

Don't buy these. Look for labels that say 'ozone safe'.

Many washing powders and cleaners are full of chemicals that are poisonous or dangerous.

Look for cleaning materials that are friendly to the environment.

Why recycle?

Many of the things we use every day are made from precious raw materials from the environment. These will run out one day, so we must not waste them. We should try to re-use them.

Recycling also reduces the amount of rubbish we have to get rid of. Most rubbish has to be buried in enormous holes in the ground called 'landfill sites'.

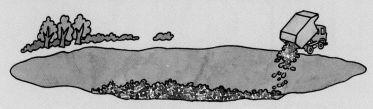

Recycling saves energy. It takes less fuel to make new things out of old ones, instead of starting from scratch.

Topsy and Tim helped pack the old bottles and newspapers in the car. Then they set off for the supermarket. The bottles clinked and chinked all the way there.

The bottle-bank stood in the supermarket car-park, next to the newspaper-bank. Dad parked the car beside them. Mummy lifted Topsy up to drop the bottles into the bottle-bank. Smash went the bottles as she dropped them in.

"Oh dear!" said Tim. "They won't be able to use those again."

"It doesn't matter," said Dad. "All the glass will be recycled to make nice new bottles."

What happens next?

1. The glass from the bottle-bank goes to the recycling factory.

2. It is unloaded into separate piles of green, brown and clear glass.

3. Bottle tops, corks and labels are removed. Then the glass is crushed.

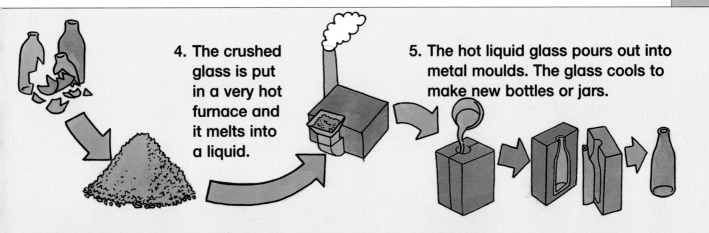

4. The crushed glass is put in a very hot furnace and it melts into a liquid.

5. The hot liquid glass pours out into metal moulds. The glass cools to make new bottles or jars.

Make your own paper

You will need:
a bowl, newspaper,
a spoon, an old pair of
tights, a lid from an empty
plastic ice-cream box, a
rolling pin and a blunt knife.

1. Tear up the newspaper into tiny pieces and soak them in a bowl of water for at least ten minutes.

2. Stir the mixture into a pulp using the spoon.

3. Ask a grown-up to make lots of holes in the plastic ice-cream lid and then

stretch the tights over the lid, making a kind of mesh.

Next Mummy and Dad posted the newspapers into the newspaper-bank. "They will be recycled as clean paper and cardboard," said Mummy.
"Paper is made from chopped-down trees, so using old paper saves lots of trees," said Dad.
"Good," said Tim.

4. Spread the newspaper pulp in a thin layer over the lid, using the blunt knife.

5. Using the rolling pin, smooth and flatten the pulp over the lid. This will also squeeze out any extra water.

6. Leave the pulp to dry for a few hours and then gently peel it off the mesh.

7. And there is your first piece of hand-made paper.

Inside the supermarket Mummy and Dad read the labels on all the things they were buying.

"These toilet rolls are made from recycled paper," said Mummy. "That will save a few trees."

Recycling paper

1. Don't waste paper – re-use it as much as possible.
2. Use both sides of writing paper.
3. Open envelopes carefully to re-use them.
4. Collect white paper from schools and offices to recycle. This is more valuable than newspaper.
5. Buy things made from recycled paper. Look out for this symbol.

Mummy chose free-range eggs for Topsy and Tim's breakfast.

"These were laid by happy hens," she said.

"Aren't all hens happy?" asked Topsy.

"No," said Mummy. "Some hens spend their whole lives shut up in tiny cages."

Topsy felt sad for those poor hens.

Help the hens

In Britain we each eat 200 eggs a year. Most of these come from hens who spend their lives shut up in cages with no room to move. They are called 'battery' hens.

Do not buy these eggs. Help to save 45 million battery hens.

To be happy, a hen likes to move around outside, pecking at the ground. We call this free-range.

Eat organic

Organic farms are places where crops are grown without using chemical fertilizers and weed-killers. The soil is kept healthy with manure and compost, and this makes the food taste better.

Animals have plenty of space to move around and natural good things to eat.

Try eating organic fruit and vegetables. Do they taste better?

Dad looked at the labels on the vegetables. "These are organic carrots," he said. "They will taste good." "What's organic, Dad?" asked Tim. "It means they have been grown without chemicals or weed-killers on them," said Dad.

Mummy bought Topsy and Tim a can of orange drink each.
They were so thirsty that they drank it all before they got
back to the car.
"Is there a rubbish bin for our cans?" asked Topsy.
"Better than that," said Mummy. "There's an Ali-bank for
cans over there."

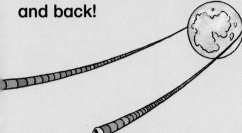

Topsy and Tim popped their empty cans into the Ali-bank.
"They'll be melted down and made into new cans," said Topsy.
"And we'll buy another drink in them next week," said Tim.

On the way home they stopped at a garage to buy some petrol.
"Miss Terry says cars are very bad," said Tim.
"They make the air all smelly and yucky," said Topsy.

The Greenhouse effect

Cars, lorries and buses burn fuel to make them go.

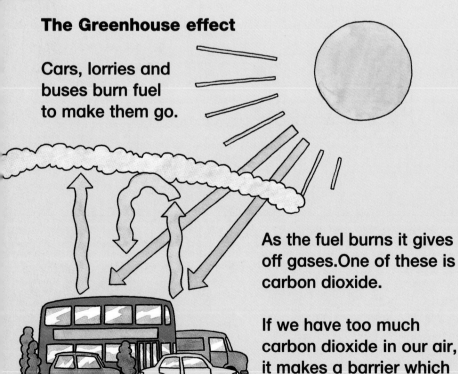

As the fuel burns it gives off gases. One of these is carbon dioxide.

If we have too much carbon dioxide in our air, it makes a barrier which traps in the sun's heat. The earth becomes like a greenhouse. The sun's heat comes in, but it can't get out again. This means that the temperature around us will get hotter and hotter. This is called global warming.

If the earth gets too warm, the ice at the North and South Poles will melt. This will make our seas much deeper and so they will flood many parts of the land.

Share a car

You can help by not using a car at all, or by using it less. Try sharing a car with friends when going to school or shopping.

Cars, buses and lorries burn up fuel which poisons the air we breathe.

Walking or cycling to school makes you fit and helps to keep the air clean.

"Well, we put lead-free petrol in our car," said Mummy. "That's not so bad to breathe, but perhaps we ought to stop using the car so much."

"We always walk to school," said Tim.

"I suppose I could bike to work," said Dad.

When they got home Topsy and Tim went out to play in the garden. "I wish we had a wild-life garden, like the one at school, so that we can help wild animals," said Topsy.
"With a pond for frogs," said Tim.
"And wild flowers for bees and butterflies," said Topsy.

A wild-life garden

This is a garden which encourages all kinds of birds, insects and creepy-crawlies to come and visit.

A wild-life garden has flowers that attract bees and butterflies, and long grasses where birds and insects can nest or hide.

The wild-life that visits the garden will feel safe because a wild-life gardener does not use chemical sprays to poison the flowers or soil.

Dad came out to cut the grass.

"Dad," said Topsy, "could we have a corner of the garden just for wild-life?"

"What sort of wild-life?" asked Dad. "Bears and gorillas?"

"No, Dad," laughed Tim. "Little wild things, like butterflies and ladybirds."

"Hmmm!" said Dad. "Ladybirds are good for the garden. They eat up pests, like greenflies."
"You wouldn't need to cut the grass in the wild-life corner," said Topsy.
"Yes, I think a wild-life corner is a great idea!" said Dad.

Mummy thought it was a good idea too.
"We ought to have a pond in our wild-life garden. Wild
things need water to drink or to swim in," said Tim.
Mummy went indoors and came back with their old baby
bath.
"This will make a good little pond for your wild-life garden,"
she said.

Mummy helped Topsy and Tim dig a hole in a sunny corner of the garden.

Make a pond

1. Ask an adult if you can make a pond in your garden. Dig a hole so that it is shallow towards the edges, but at least 40 cm deep near the middle.

2. Line the hole with old newspapers, carpet underlay or sand.

3. Cover this with polythene or PVC sheeting. Now slowly fill the pond with water.

4. When it is full, put stones, turf or earth around the edges.

They put the baby bath in the hole and Topsy and Tim carried water to it in their old seaside buckets.

Topsy planted a tuft of grass in a flowerpot and stood it in the middle of the pond. "That's a little island for the wild-life," she said.

Pond life

You can put a layer of earth in the bottom of your pond for plants to grow in. Put water-loving plants around the edge of the pond.

After a while your pond will attract frogs, newts, birds and all sorts of insects.

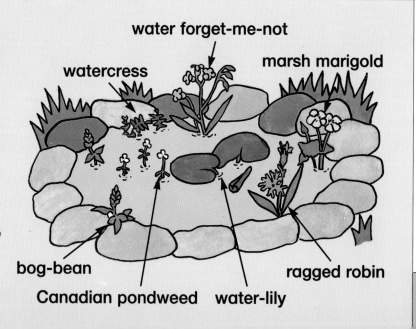

water forget-me-not

watercress

marsh marigold

bog-bean

Canadian pondweed   water-lily

ragged robin

Spot the visitor

Sit quietly by the pond in your garden, or lie in the grass, keeping very still. Watch closely for the tiny creatures that run to and fro. Listen to the sounds. How many different insects can you see? How many birds? Write them down in a notebook. Can you draw them?

After lunch Topsy and Tim went out to look for wild things in their garden. Topsy saw them first – three bees on the island in the pond.

"Look," said Tim. "They're drinking the water."

"They like our wild-life garden," said Topsy.

Ways to help wild-life

Make a wild-life garden like Topsy and Tim's

Leave grass, dandelions, nettles and thistles to grow long at the end of the garden.

Hedgehog hints

If you spot a hedgehog in your garden, leave out a saucer filled with dog or cat food. Hedgehogs need to fatten up in the autumn to get them through the winter months. Never give milk to a hedgehog.

Flowers and trees

Plant flowers like lavender, wallflowers, buddleia, or honeysuckle. They are full of nectar to attract bees and butterflies.

Buy a packet of wild flower seeds such as bluebell, primrose, campion and lady-smock.

Plant rowan and crab-apple trees to attract birds.

Bluebell

Primrose

Lavender

Honeysuckle

Make a compost heap

Compost is a new soil made from old rotted down vegetable remains. Many gardeners make their own compost, because it is very good for the soil.

You can save fruit and vegetable scraps to put on your compost heap.

Help the birds

Feeding

Leave food out for the birds between October and April. They can find their own for the rest of the year. Birds need feeding every day in the winter. Most birds love seed cake.

Other bird treats:

Meaty bone/unsalted peanuts/stale cheese/stale cake and bread/bacon rind/chicken skin.

When baby birds start to hatch in the spring, it is time to stop leaving out food. Our foods give baby birds stomach-ache.

Cold weather cake recipe

Left-over bread
Cake crumbs
Cooked potato
Currants
Bird seed
Bacon rind, chopped

MIX with cool, melted fat.
Leave to set.

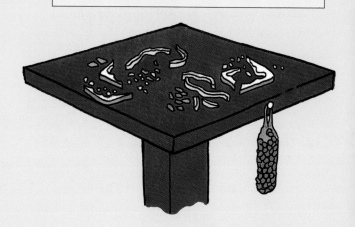

Never give birds salted peanuts.

Water

Birds need water for drinking and bathing all year round. Fill an old dustbin lid or pie dish with fresh water each day. Keep it free of ice in winter.

Nesting

Birds make their nests from bits of moss, animal hair and dry grass.

Hang out a bag with bits of wool and fluffy things to help the birds line their nests.

Put a nesting box somewhere safe. Watch to see if a bird makes its home there.

Robins sometimes build their nests in funny places.

Sparrows make untidy nests.

Never touch a nest or steal birds' eggs.

Topsy and Tim follow the Country Code

When you go into the countryside there are some rules you should try to remember.

1. Guard against fire.

2. Fasten gates.

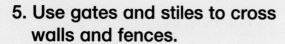

3. Keep dogs under control.

4. Keep to public paths across farmland.

5. Use gates and stiles to cross walls and fences.

6. Take your litter home.

7. Don't damage or pick plants.

8. Don't dirty rivers, ponds or lakes.

9. Don't make a loud noise.

Word List

Ali-bank

a large container, where you can put used aluminium cans. These are then taken away to be recycled.

aluminium

a very light metal that never rusts, so it is easy to recycle.

bauxite

a soft rock found in the ground. It is used to make aluminium.

CFCs

these three letters are short for the word chlorofluorocarbons. These are chemicals which destroy the ozone layer. Our fridges, freezers and aerosol sprays give off CFCs.

compost

a mixture of organic remains such as tea leaves, potato peelings, grass cuttings.

environment

our surroundings.

green

a word used to describe the many ways of caring for the enviroment.

landfill site

a very large hole in the ground, into which rubbish is tipped.

organic

something that comes from living plants and animals, such as manure and dead leaves. Crops that are grown organically are grown in soil fertilized with manure or compost.

ozone layer

ozone is a gas which forms a layer around the earth. This later stops dangerous rays from the sun reaching us and harming our skin.

pesticide

a chemical which is used to kill insects and creatures that damage farmers' crops. Pesticides are dangerous because they sometimes destroy more than just the pest.

pollute

to damage the surroundings that we live in. We can do this in many ways by dropping litter, or by dumping rubbish and poisonous chemicals.

raw materials

these are natural things that we can get from the earth on which we live. These materials include wood from trees, oil and precious metals from under the ground.

recycle

to re-use materials over and over again.

steel

this is a metal made from iron. It is called an alloy, as it is mixed with other metals.

tropical rainforest

large forests around the middle of the Earth where it is hot all year. Tropical rainforests contain thousands of different kinds of tree, flower and animal. They help to keep the earth's air clean.